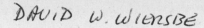

PENGUIN BOOKS

THE WRITER'S QUOTATION BOOK

James Charlton lives in Greenwich Village, New York. He is the editor of many books, including *The Writer's Home Companion* (also available from Penguin).

THE
WRITER'S
QUOTATION
BOOK

A LITERARY COMPANION

PENGUIN BOOKS

EDITED BY
JAMES CHARLTON

PENGUIN BOOKS
Published by the Penguin Group
Viking Penguin, a division of Penguin Books USA Inc.,
375 Hudson Street, New York, New York 10014, U.S.A.
Penguin Books Ltd, 27 Wrights Lane, London W8 5TZ, England
Penguin Books Australia Ltd, Ringwood, Victoria, Australia
Penguin Books Canada Ltd, 10 Alcorn Avenue, Suite 300,
Toronto, Ontario, Canada M4V 3B2
Penguin Books (N.Z.) Ltd, 182–190 Wairau Road,
Auckland 10, New Zealand

Penguin Books Ltd, Registered Offices:
Harmondsworth, Middlesex, England

First published in the United States of America by
Pushcart Press 1991
Published in Penguin Books 1992

3 5 7 9 10 8 6 4 2

ISBN 0 14 01.6683 1

(CIP data available)

Printed in the United States of America
Designed by Hudson Studio

In *Travels with My Aunt,* Graham Greene wrote that "people who like quotes like meaningless generalizations." I plead guilty. But as I write this, the third introduction to *The Writer's Quotation Book,* there must be a number of other people who share my guilt. Writers love quotations. They love quoting someone else's work almost as much as they love quoting their own. It is the sign of a well-read person to be able to drop a quote from Shakespeare, Twain or Marx—Groucho or Karl—into a conversation.

The Writer's Quotation Book has been in print in its various editions—domestic, foreign, book club and Penguin paperback—for more than ten years and in that time has sold over one hundred thousand copies. Given the vagaries of contemporary publishing, with its plethora of titles, turnover of editors and endless merging of companies, the duration is a marvel to me. As any reader or, alas, writer knows, the availability of a new title is akin to the life span of a fruit fly, so to have a book last more than a season is wonder. Herbert Giles, in his *History of Chinese Literature,* mentions a statesman during the Han Dynasty, about 13 B.C, who had a unique way of encouraging new books and writers; all existing books were ordered burned so that literature might start anew. A bit drastic, but it is a way of helping the publication of new titles.

It is very satisfying for a writer or editor to write an introduction to the third edition of *anything*, let alone a book as enjoyable to me as this one is. It of course is no classic in a literary sense, but a classic, as defined by Mark Twain, is "something that everyone wants to have read and nobody wants to read." Much like salted peanuts before a meal, this small volume is here merely to amuse the reader before he sits down with a novel, or inspire the writer before she must face a blank screen or sheet of paper.

This new, revised and expanded third edition of *The Writer's Quotation Book* again owes a great deal to the readers who sent along clippings, interviews, quotes and suggestions. This third edition is larger by far than the earlier two though it is, by design, not encyclopedic. Every quote is here, I hope, because it strikes a chord in a reader. I think all readers, writers, and their friends will find this book amusing, entertaining, and instructive.

JIM CHARLTON
New York City

THE WRITER'S QUOTATION BOOK

Literature was not born the day when a boy crying "wolf, wolf" came running out of the Neanderthal valley with a big gray wolf at his heels: literature was born on the day when a boy came crying "wolf, wolf" and there was no wolf behind him.
VLADIMIR NABOKOV

The last thing that we find in making a book is to know what we must put first.
BLAISE PASCAL

There is nothing so important as the book can be.
MAXWELL PERKINS

All that Mankind has done, thought, gained or been: it is lying as in magic preservation in the pages of books. They are the chosen possession of man.
THOMAS CARLYLE

It is a great thing to start life with a small number of really good books which are your very own.
SHERLOCK HOLMES

The walls of books around him, dense with the past, formed a kind of insulation against the present world and its disasters.
ROSS MACDONALD

A room without books is like a body without soul.
CICERO

As good almost kill a man as kill a good book: who kills a man kills a reasonable creature, God's image; but he who destroys a good book kills reason itself, kills the image of God, as it were, in the eye.
JOHN MILTON

An ordinary man can ... surround himself with two thousand books ... and thenceforward have at least one place in the world in which it is possible to be happy.
AUGUSTINE BIRRELL

Only one hour in the normal day is more pleasurable than the hour spent in bed with a book before going to sleep, and that is the hour spent in bed with a book after being called in the morning.
ROSE MACAULAY

The pleasure of all reading is doubled when one lives with another who shares the same books.
KATHERINE MANSFIELD

Books are a delightful society. If you go into a room filled with books, even without taking them down from their shelves, they seem to speak to you, to welcome you.
WILLIAM E. GLADSTONE

Books are not made for furniture, but there is nothing else that so beautifully furnishes a house.
HENRY WARD BEECHER

The harmonies of bound books are like the flowers of the field.
HILAIRE BELLOC

There are books which I love to see on the shelf. I feel a virtue goes out of them, but I should think it undue familiarity to read them.
SAMUEL MC CHORD CROTHERS

Everywhere I have sought rest and found it not except sitting apart in a nook with a little book.
THOMAS À KEMPIS

Just the knowledge that a good book is waiting one at the end of a long day makes that day happier.
KATHLEEN NORRIS

Some say life is the thing, but I prefer reading.
RUTH RENDELL

If you cannot read all your books, at any rate handle, or as it were, fondle them—peer into them, let them fall open where they will, read from the first sentence that arrests the eye, set them back on the shelves with your own hands, arrange them on your own plan so that you at least know where they are. Let them be your friends; let them at any rate be your acquaintances.
WINSTON CHURCHILL

Americans like fat books and thin women.
RUSSELL BAKER

I can't wait to run against a President who owns more tuxedos than books.
SENATOR GARY HART

There is no doubt in my mind that, should we have been choosing our leaders on the basis of their reading experience and not their political programs, there would be much less grief on earth.
JOSEPH BRODSKY

Only the man who is wide awake is capable of enjoying a book, of extracting from it what is vital. Such a man enjoys whatever comes into his experience and, unless I am horribly mistaken, makes no distinction between the experiences offered through reading and the manifold experiences of everyday life.
HENRY MILLER

If you understand everything you have read in your life, you would already know what you are looking for now.
GEORGES GURDJIEFF

In a very real sense, people who have read good literature have lived more than people who cannot or will not read. . . . It is not true that we have only one life to live; if we can read, we can live as many more lives and as many kinds of lives as we wish.
S. I. HAYAKAWA

It is a mistake to think that books have come to stay.
The human race did without them for thousands of
years and may decide to do without them again.

E. M. FORSTER

The world, you must remember, is only just becoming
literate.

ALDOUS HUXLEY

This will never be a civilized country until we expend
more money for books than we do for chewing gum.

ELBERT HUBBARD

The public which reads, in any sense of the word
worth considering, is very, very small; the public
which would feel no lack if all book-printing ceased
tomorrow is enormous.

GEORGE GISSING

The man who does not read good books has no advantage over the man who can't read them.

MARK TWAIN

It is absurd to have a hard-and-fast rule about what
one should read and what one shouldn't. More than
half of modern culture depends on what one shouldn't
read.

OSCAR WILDE

Books are fatal: they are the curse of the human race. Nine-tenths of existing books are nonsense, and the clever books are the refutation of that nonsense. The greatest misfortune that ever befell man was the invention of printing.

BENJAMIN DISRAELI

Books are a medium because they're neither rare nor well done.

GORE VIDAL

In literature, as in love, we are astonished at what is chosen by others.

ANDRE MAUROIS

Sir, the fact that a book is in the public library brings no comfort. Books are the one element in which I am personally and nakedly acquisitive. If it weren't for the law I would steal them. If it weren't for my purse I would buy them.

HAROLD LASKI

Never lend books, for no one ever returns them; the only books I have in my library are books that other folk have lent me.

ANATOLE FRANCE

Your borrower of books—those mutilators of collections, spoilers of the symmetry of shelves, and creators of odd volumes.

CHARLES LAMB

When I get a little money, I buy books; and if any is left, I buy food and clothes.

DESIDERIUS ERASMUS

Hard-covered books break up friendships. You loan a hard-covered book to a friend and when he doesn't return it you get mad at him. It makes you mean and petty. But twenty-five cent books are different.

JOHN STEINBECK

The multitude of books is making us ignorant.

VOLTAIRE

There are times when I think that the reading I have done in the past has had no effect except to cloud my mind and make me indecisive.

ROBERTSON DAVIES

If we encounter a man of rare intellect, we should ask him what books he reads.

RALPH WALDO EMERSON

If I read a book that impresses me, I have to take myself firmly in hand before I mix with other people; otherwise they would think my mind rather queer.

ANNE FRANK

Read as many of the great books as you can before the age of 22.

JAMES MICHENER

We live in an age that reads too much to be wise.
OSCAR WILDE

The ratio of literacy to illiteracy is constant, but now-adays the illiterates can read.
ALBERTO MORAVIA

There is more treasure in books than in all the pirates' loot on Treasure Island ... and best of all, you can enjoy these riches every day of your life.
WALT DISNEY

A book is like a garden carried in the pocket.
CHINESE PROVERB

Reading is to the mind what exercise is to the body.
SIR RICHARD STEELE

The best effect of any book is that it excites the reader to self-activity.
THOMAS CARLYLE

A man may as well expect to grow stronger by always eating as wiser by always reading.
JEREMY COLLIER

I would never read a book if it were possible for me to talk half an hour with the man who wrote it.
WOODROW WILSON

There are, in actual fact, men who talk like books. Happily, however, there are also books that talk like men.

THEODOR HAECKER

There are no bad books, any more than there are ugly women.

ANATOLE FRANCE

No woman was ever ruined by a book.

JIMMY WALKER, Mayor of New York City

Those whom books will hurt will not be proof against events. If some books are deemed more baneful and their sale forbid how, then, with deadlier facts, not dreams of doting men? Events, not books, should be forbid.

HERMAN MELVILLE

There is a great deal of difference between an eager man who wants to read a book and a tired man who wants a book to read.

G. K. CHESTERTON

I divide all readers into two classes; those who read to remember and those who read to forget.

WILLIAM LYON PHELPS

One old lady who wants her head lifted wouldn't be so bad, but you multiply her two hundred and fifty thousand times and what you get is a book club.

FLANNERY O'CONNOR

As a rule reading fiction is as hard to me as trying to hit a target by hurling feathers at it. I need resistance to cerebrate!

WILLIAM JAMES

No man understands a deep book until he has seen and lived at least part of its contents.

EZRA POUND

A book is a mirror; if an ass peers into it, you can't expect an apostle to peer out.

GEORG CHRISTOPH LICHTENBERG

When you reread a classic you do not see more in the book than you did before; you see more in you than was there before.

CLIFTON FADIMAN

The art of reading is in great part that of acquiring a better understanding of life from one's encounter with it in a book.

ANDRE MAUROIS

I suggest that the only books that influenced us are those for which we are ready, and which have gone a little farther down our particular path than we have yet gone ourselves.

E. M. FORSTER

There are some books one needs maturity to enjoy just as there are books an adult can come upon too late to savor.

PHYLLIS MC GINLEY

No book is really worth reading at the age of ten which is not equally (and often far more) worth reading at the age of fifty and beyond.

C. S. LEWIS

The stories of childhood leave an indelible impression, and their author always has a niche in the temple of memory from which the image is never cut out to be thrown on the rubbish heap of things that are outgrown and outlived.

HOWARD PYLE

The road to ignorance is paved with good editions.

GEORGE BERNARD SHAW

Every man who knows how to read has it in his power to magnify himself, to multiply the ways in which he exists, to make his life full, significant and interesting.

ALDOUS HUXLEY

When we read too fast or too slowly, we understand nothing.

BLAISE PASCAL

Who knows if Shakespeare might not have thought less if he had read more.
EDWARD YOUNG

Where is human nature so weak as in the bookstore?
HENRY WARD BEECHER

The oldest books are still only just out to those who have not read them.
SAMUEL BUTLER

The worst thing about new books is that they keep us from reading the old ones.
JOSEPH JOUBERT

Never read any book that is not a year old.
RALPH WALDO EMERSON

There is a good saying to the effect that when a new book appears one should read an old one. As an author I would not recommend too strict an adherence to this saying.
WINSTON CHURCHILL

A professional writer is an amateur who didn't quit.
RICHARD BACH

A hack is on the constant hunt for 'ideas' for his plots or 'new angles.' The real writer is haunted by a plot which he must write out of inner necessity. He is impervious to suggestions.
EDMUND BERGLER

The writer comes up against the misconception that he's needed only for his manual ability to translate other people's experience into words. The non-writer's illusion is, "I am just as good, I have just as much to say, more to say, but I'm missing a few technical details."

ERNEST VAN DER HAAG

What they [the amateurs] are really saying is "I have a story and I want it told." This compulsion is what enables the journalist to get his information. It's the writer's job to flesh out the stories he hears.

TOM WOLFE

I think it can be dangerous for young writers to be modest when they're young. I've known a number of truly talented writers who did less than they could have done because they weren't vain and unpleasant enough about their talent. You have to take it seriously.

NORMAN MAILER

Of course no writers ever forget their first acceptance. . . . One fine day when I was seventeen I had my first, second and third, all in the same morning's mail. Oh, I'm here to tell you, dizzy with excitement is no mere phrase!

TRUMAN CAPOTE

Publication—is the auction of the Mind of Man.
EMILY DICKINSON

For several days after my first book was published I carried it about in my pocket, and took surreptitious peeps at it to make sure the ink had not faded.
SIR JAMES M. BARRIE

I don't keep any copy of my books around. . . . They would embarrass me. When I finish writing my books, I kick them in the belly, and have done with them.
LUDWIG BEMELMANS

I am very foolish over my own book. I have a copy which I constantly read and find very illuminating. Swift confesses to something of the sort with his own compositions.
J. B. YEATS in a letter to his son, W. B. YEATS

If there is a special Hell for writers it would be in the forced contemplation of their own works, with all the misconceptions, the omissions, the failures that any finished work of art implies.
JOHN DOS PASSOS

On the day when a young writer corrects his first proofsheet he is as proud as a schoolboy who has just gotten his first dose of the pox.
CHARLES BAUDELAIRE

Most of the basic material a writer works with is acquired before the age of fifteen.

WILLA CATHER

However great a man's natural talent may be, the art of writing cannot be learned all at once.

JEAN JACQUES ROUSSEAU

When I was twenty I was in love with words, a wordsmith. I didn't know enough to know when people were letting words get in their way. Now I like the words to disappear, like a transparent curtain.

WALLACE STEGNER

By reading what he has last written, just before he recommences his task, the writer will catch the tone and spirit of what he is then saying, and will avoid the fault of seeming to be unlike himself.

ANTHONY TROLLOPE

I have never been good at revising. I always thought I made things worse by recasting and retouching. I never knew what was meant by choice of words. It was one word or none.

ROBERT FROST

I used to be adjective happy. Now I cut them with so much severity that I find I have to put a few adjectives back.

FRANK YERBY

When you catch an adjective, kill it.
MARK TWAIN

Cut out all those exclamation marks. An exclamation mark is like laughing at your own joke.
F. SCOTT FITZGERALD

As for my next book, I am going to hold myself from writing it till I have it impending in me: grown heavy in my mind like a ripe pear; pendant, gravid, asking to be cut or it will fall.
VIRGINIA WOOLF

For a dyed-in-the-wool author nothing is as dead as a book once it is written. . . . She is rather like a cat whose kittens have grown-up. While they were a-growing she was passionately interested in them but now they seem hardly to belong to her—and probably she is involved with another batch of kittens as I am involved with other writing.
RUMER GODDEN

When I read my first book, I started writing my first book. I have never not been writing.
GORE VIDAL

Looking back, I imagine I was always writing. Twaddle it was too. But better far write twaddle or anything, anything, than nothing at all.
KATHERINE MANSFIELD

I suppose I am a born novelist, for the things I imagine are more vital and vivid to me than the things I remember.

ELLEN GLASGOW

There are three reasons for becoming a writer: the first is that you need the money; the second, that you have something to say that you think the world should know; the third is that you can't think what to do with the long winter evenings.

QUENTIN CRISP

If we should ever inaugurate a hall of fame, it would be reserved exclusively and hopefully for authors who, having written four bestsellers, still refrained from starting out on a lecture tour.

E. B. WHITE

Almost all the great writers have as their motif, more or less disguised, the "passage from childhood to maturity," the clash between the thrill of expectation, and the disillusioning knowledge of the truth. *Lost Illusion* is the undisclosed title of every novel.

ANDRE MAUROIS

If you have to pick it after the book is done, it's like trying to buy the right wedding ring.

NORMAN MAILER, on picking a title

I'm terrible about titles; I don't know how to come up with them. They're the one thing in the story I'm really uncertain about.

EUDORA WELTY

Sometimes people give titles to me, and sometimes I see them on a billboard.

ROBERT PENN WARREN

A good title should be like a good metaphor; it should intrigue without being too baffling or too obvious.

WALKER PERCY

There are some books of which scores of copies are bought for one which is read, and others which have dozens of readers for every copy sold.

JOHN AYSCOUGH

What a sense of superiority it gives one to escape reading a book which everyone else is reading.

ALICE JAMES

One always tends to overpraise a long book, because one has got through it.

E. M. FORSTER

There are two motives for reading a book; one, that you enjoy it; the other, that you can boast about it.

BERTRAND RUSSELL

Have you not noticed, after many heartaches and disillusionments, that in recommending a book to a friend the less said the better? The moment you praise a book too highly you awaken resistance in your listener.

HENRY MILLER

Some writers thrive with the contact with the commerce of success; others are corrupted by it. Perhaps, like losing one's virginity it is not as bad (or as good) as one feared it was going to be.

V. S. PRITCHETT

Best-Sellerism is the star system of the book world. A "best-seller" is a celebrity among books. It is known primarily (sometimes exclusively) for its well-knownness.

DANIEL J. BOORSTIN   *The Image (?)*

There are books and there is literature. I have never met anyone who bought a book on the bestseller lists.

ELIZABETH HARDWICK

All literature, all art, best seller or worst, must be sincere, if it is to be successful. . . . Only a person with a Best Seller mind can write Best Sellers; and only someone with a mind like Shelley's can write *Prometheus Unbound*. The deliberate forger has little chance with his contemporaries and none at all with posterity.

ALDOUS HUXLEY

A best-seller is the gilded tomb of a mediocre talent.
LOGAN PEARSALL SMITH

Usually the recipe for a bestseller is to give people
what they want. My challenge is and was: Give them
what they do not expect. Be severe with them. The
world of media is full of easy answers, wash-and-wear
philosophies, instant ecstasies, what-me-worry Epiph-
anies. Probably readers want a little more.
UMBERTO ECO

The secret of popular writing is never to put more
on a given page than the common reader can lap off
it with no strain whatsoever on his habitually slack
attention.
EZRA POUND

I'm a lousy writer; a helluva lot of people have got
lousy taste.
GRACE METALIOUS

Those big-shot writers... could never dig the fact
that there are more salted peanuts consumed than
caviar.
MICKEY SPILLANE

I try to leave out the parts that people skip.
ELMORE LEONARD

Almost anyone can be an author; the business is to collect money and fame from this state of being.

A. A. MILNE

Writing is the only profession where no one considers you ridiculous if you earn no money.

JULES RENARD

Sir, no man but a blockhead ever wrote except for money.

SAMUEL JOHNSON

Write without pay until somebody offers pay. If nobody offers pay within three years, the candidate may look upon this circumstance with the most implicit confidence as the sign that sawing wood is what he was intended for.

MARK TWAIN

The profession of book-writing makes horse racing seem like a solid, stable business.

JOHN STEINBECK

If writers were good businessmen, they'd have too much sense to be writers.

IRVIN S. COBB

The multitude of books is a great evil. There is no measure of limit to this fever of writing; everyone must be an author, some for some kind of vanity to acquire celebrity and raise a name, others for the sake of lucre or gain.

MARTIN LUTHER

I do think that the quality which makes a man want to write and be read is essentially a desire for self-exposure and is masochistic. Like one of those guys who has a compulsion to take his thing out and show it on the street.

JAMES JONES

I don't want to take up literature in a money-making spirit, or be very anxious about making large profits, but selling it at a loss is another thing altogether, and an amusement I cannot well afford.

LEWIS CARROLL

One of the least impressive liberties is the liberty to starve. This particular liberty is freely accorded to authors.

LORD GOODMAN

Years ago, to say you were a writer was not the highest recommendation to your landlord. Today, he at least hesitates before he refuses to rent you an apartment—for all he knows you may be rich.

ARTHUR MILLER

When one says that a writer is fashionable one practically always means that he is admired by people under thirty.

GEORGE ORWELL

An author is a person who can never take innocent pleasure in visiting a bookstore again. Say you go in and discover that there are no copies of your book on the shelves. You resent all the other books—I don't care if they are *Great Expectations, Life on the Mississippi*, and the *King James Bible*—that are on the shelves.

ROY BLOUNT, JR.

A man really writes for an audience of about ten persons. Of course, if others like it, that is clear gain. But if those ten are satisfied, he is content.

ALFRED NORTH WHITEHEAD

I write what I would like to read—what I think other women would like to read. If what I write makes a woman in the Canadian mountains cry and she writes and tells me about it, especially if she says "I read it to Tom when he came in from work and he cried too," I feel I have succeeded.

KATHLEEN NORRIS, on the publication of her seventy-eighth book.

When I was a ten-year-old book worm and used to kiss the dust jacket pictures of authors as if they were icons, it used to amaze me that these remote people could provoke me to love.

ERICA JONG

Anything that is written to please the author is worthless.

BLAISE PASCAL

Any writer overwhelmingly honest about pleasing himself is almost sure to please others.

MARIANNE MOORE

My purpose is to entertain myself first and other people secondly.

JOHN D. MACDONALD

I write in order to attain that feeling of tension relieved and function achieved which a cow enjoys on giving milk.

H. L. MENCKEN

When I write, I aim in my mind not toward New York but a vague spot a little east of Kansas. I think of the books on library shelves, without their jackets, years old, and a countryish teen-aged boy finding them, and having them speak to him. The reviews, the stacks in Brentano's are just hurdles to get over, to place the books on that shelf.

JOHN UPDIKE

Your audience is one single reader. I have found that sometimes it helps to pick out one person—a real person you know, or an imagined person and write to that one.

JOHN STEINBECK

A kid is a guy I never wrote down to. He's interested in what I say if I make it interesting. He is also the last container of a sense of humor, which disappears as he gets older, and he laughs only according to the way the boss, society, politics, or race want him to. Then he becomes an adult. An adult is an obsolete child.

THEODORE GEISEL (Dr. Seuss)

People want to know why I do this, why I write such gross stuff. I like to tell them I have the heart of a small boy—and I keep it in a jar on my desk.

STEPHEN KING

I do not believe the expenditure of $2.50 for a book entitles the purchaser to the personal friendship of the author.

EVELYN WAUGH

Writing is one of the few professions left where you take all the responsibility for what you do. It's really dangerous and ultimately destroys you as a writer if you start thinking about responses to your work or what your audience needs.

ERICA JONG

There are two basic reactions. There are those who hate you because they think you put them in your book, and there are those who hate you because they think you didn't put them in your book.

HANIF KUREISHI

If you caricature friends in your first novel they will be upset, but if you don't they will feel betrayed.

MORDECAI RICHLER

When I'm writing I'm always aware that this friend is going to like this, or that another friend is going to like that paragraph or chapter, always thinking of specific people. In the end all books are written for your friends.

GABRIEL GARCIA MARQUEZ

Writers, if they are worthy of that jealous designation, do not write for other writers. They write to give reality to experience.

ARCHIBALD MACLEISH

My yesterdays walk with me. They keep step, they are gray faces that peer over my shoulder.

WILLIAM GOLDING

In a very real sense, the writer writes in order to teach himself, to understand himself, to satisfy himself; the publishing of his ideas, though it brings gratifications, is a curious anticlimax.

ALFRED KAZIN

No wonder the really powerful men in our society, whether politicians or scientists, hold writers and poets in contempt. They do it because they get no evidence from modern literature that anybody is thinking about any significant question.

SAUL BELLOW

America is about the last place in which life will be endurable at all for an inspired writer.

SAMUEL BUTLER

In America only the successful writer is important, in France all writers are important, in England no writer is important, in Australia you have to explain what a writer is.

GEOFFREY COTTERELL

A Frenchman can humiliate an Englishman just as readily as an Englishman can humiliate an American, and an American a Canadian. One of Canada's most serious literary needs is some lesser nation to domineer over and shame by displays of superior taste.

ROBERTSON DAVIES

Why has the South produced so many good writers? Because we got beat.

WALKER PERCY

When I'm asked why Southern writers particularly have a penchant for writing about freaks, I say it's because we are still able to recognize one.

FLANNERY O'CONNOR

My mother, Southern to the bone, once told me, "All Southern literature can be summed up in these words: 'On the night the hogs ate Willie, Mama died when she heard what Daddy did to Sister.'" She raised me up to be a Southern writer, but it wasn't easy.

PAT CONROY

To write is to write is to write is to write is to write is to write is to write is to write.

GERTRUDE STEIN

Nothing in language is immutably fixed: the best writers are constantly changing it. Absolute government by dictionary would mean the arrest of this healthy process of change and growth.

C. E. MONTAGUE

Word has somehow got around that the split infinitive is always wrong. That is a piece with the outworn notion that it is always wrong to strike a lady.

JAMES THURBER

Would you convey my compliments to the purist who reads your proofs and tell him or her that I write in a sort of broken-down patois which is something like the way a Swiss waiter talks, and that when I split an infinitive, God dammit, I split it so it will stay split.

RAYMOND CHANDLER

A man who writes well writes not as others write, but as he himself writes; it is often in speaking badly that he speaks well.

MONTESQUIEU

A poet never takes notes. You never take notes in a love affair.

ROBERT FROST

Aphorisms are bad for novels. They stick in the reader's teeth.

ANATOLE BROYARD

The difference between the right word and the nearly right word is the same as that between lightning and the lightning bug.

MARK TWAIN

I am going to be vague expressly; I could be altogether explicit, but it is not my intention to be so. For once a thing is defined, it is dead.

KRISHNAMURTI

I think to be oversensitive about cliches is like being oversensitive about table manners.

EVELYN WAUGH

I often think how much easier life would have been for me and how much time I would have saved if I had known the alphabet. I can never tell where I and J stand without saying G, H to myself first. I don't know whether P comes before R or after, and where T comes in has to this day remained something that I have never been able to get into my head.

W. SOMERSET MAUGHAM

It's not the most intellectual job in the world, but I do have to know the letters.

VANNA WHITE

In conversation you can use timing, a look, inflection, pauses. But on the page all you have is commas, dashes, the amount of syllables in a word. When I write I read everything out loud to get the right rhythm.

FRAN LEBOWITZ

I don't enjoy writing, and I certainly would not do it for a living. Some people do, but some people enjoy flagellation.

PRINCE PHILIP, DUKE OF EDINBURGH

Writing is easy; all you do is sit staring at a blank sheet of paper until the drops of blood form on your forehead.

GENE FOWLER

There's nothing to writing. All you do is sit down at a typewriter and open a vein.

RED SMITH

I lost everything at Philippi, and took to poetry to make a living, but now I have a competence I should be mad if I did not prefer ease to writing.

HORACE

When I stepped from hard manual work to writing, I just stepped from one kind of hard work to another.

SEAN O'CASEY

If you are getting the worst of it in an argument with a literary man, always attack his style. That'll touch him if nothing else will.

J. A. SPENDER

In stating as fully as I could how things really were, it was often very difficult and I wrote awkwardly and the awkwardness is what they called my style. All mistakes and awkwardness are easy to see, and they called it style.

ERNEST HEMINGWAY

You can be a little ungrammatical if you come from the right part of the country.
ROBERT FROST

I can't write five words but that I change seven.
DOROTHY PARKER

I have written—often several times—every word I have ever published. My pencils outlast their erasures.
VLADIMIR NABOKOV

Nothing you write, if you hope to be any good, will ever come out as you first hoped.
LILLIAN HELLMAN

I quit writing if I feel inspired, because I know I'm going to have to throw it away. Writing a novel is like building a wall brick by brick; only amateurs believe in inspiration.
FRANK YERBY

There are days when the result is so bad that no fewer than five revisions are required. In contrast, when I'm greatly inspired, only four revisions are needed.
JOHN KENNETH GALBRAITH

I believe more in the scissors than I do in the pencil.
TRUMAN CAPOTE

I hate to write; I like to revise. And the amount of revision I do is terrific. I like to get the first draft out of my system. That's the hardest thing for me.

MALCOLM COWLEY

The most essential gift for a good writer is a built-in shockproof shit-detector.

ERNEST HEMINGWAY

You will have to write and put away or burn a lot of material before you are comfortable in this medium. You might as well start now and get the necessary work done. For I believe that eventually quantity will make for quality.

RAY BRADBURY

I write whenever it suits me. During a creative period I write every day; a novel should not be interrupted. When I cease to be carried along, when I no longer feel as though I were taking down dictation, I stop.

FRANCOIS MAURIAC

I write a lot—every day, seven days a week—and I throw a lot away. Sometimes I think I write to throw away; it's a process of distillation.

DONALD BARTHELME

The wastepaper basket is the writer's best friend.
ISAAC B. SINGER

Read over your compositions and, when you meet a passage which you think is particularly fine, strike it out.
SAMUEL JOHNSON

What I had to face, the very bitter lesson that everyone who wants to write has got to learn, was that a thing may in itself be the finest piece of writing one has ever done, and yet have absolutely no place in the manuscript one hopes to publish.
THOMAS WOLFE

To write simply is as difficult as to be good.
W. SOMERSET MAUGHAM

We like that a sentence should read as if its author, had he held a plough instead of a pen, could have drawn a furrow deep and straight to the end.
HENRY DAVID THOREAU

Often I think writing is a sheer paring away of oneself leaving always something thinner, barer, more meager.
F. SCOTT FITZGERALD

A bad book is as much a labor to write as a good one; it comes as sincerely from the author's soul.

ALDOUS HUXLEY

I'm not sure a bad person can write a good book. If art doesn't make us better, then what on earth is it for?

ALICE WALKER

It takes less time to learn to write nobly than to learn to write lightly and straightforwardly.

FRIEDRICH WILHELM NIETZSCHE

All a writer has to do is get a woman to say he's a writer; it's an aphrodisiac.

SAUL BELLOW

Pretty women swarm around everybody but writers. Plain, intelligent women somewhat swarm around writers.

WILLIAM SAROYAN

If you were a member of Jesse James' band and people asked you what you were, you wouldn't say, 'Well, I'm a desperado.' You'd say something like 'I work in banks' or 'I've done some railroad work.' It took me a long time just to say 'I'm a writer.' It's really embarrassing.

ROY BLOUNT, JR.

Most writers enjoy two periods of happiness—when a glorious idea comes to mind and, secondly, when a last page has been written and you haven't had time to know how much better it ought to be.

J. B. PRIESTLEY

Most writers are in a state of gloom a good deal of the time; they need perpetual reassurance.

JOHN HALL WHEELOCK

Writing is essentially a private toil. You have very few things to work with—the gifts you were born with, which nobody can change, and some ability to educate yourself in a literary way, which you must do on your own. There's only one thing that can be given externally, and that is the inspiration of praise.

CYNTHIA OZICK

It's my experience that very few writers, young or old, are really seeking advice when they give out their work to be read. They want support; they want someone to say, 'Good job.'

JOHN IRVING

Writing is not a profession but a vocation of unhappiness.

GEORGES SIMENON

Writing's not terrible, it's wonderful. I keep my own hours, do what I please. When I want to travel, I can. But mainly I'm doing what I most wanted to do all my life. I'm not into the agonies of creation.

RAYMOND CARVER

Writing a book is not as tough as it is to haul 35 people around the country and sweat like a horse five nights a week.

BETTE MIDLER

For forty-odd years in this noble profession I've harbored a guilt and my conscience is smitten. So here is my slightly embarrassed confession— I don't like to write, but I love to have written.

MICHAEL KANIN

Many people who want to be writers don't really want to be writers. They want to have been writers. They wish they had a book in print.

JAMES MICHENER

I love being a writer. What I can't stand is the paperwork.

PETER DE VRIES

Planning to write is not writing. Outlining a book is not writing. Researching is not writing. Talking to people about what you're doing, none of that is writing. Writing is writing.

E. L. DOCTOROW

It is a fact that few novelists enjoy the creative labour, though most enjoy thinking about the creative labour.

ARNOLD BENNETT

I hate writing. I will do anything to avoid it. The only way I could write less was if I was dead.

FRAN LEBOWITZ

What release to write so that one forgets oneself, forgets one's companion, forgets where one is or what one is going to do next—to be drenched in sleep or in the sea. Pencils and pads and curling blue sheets alive with letters heap up on the desk.

ANNE MORROW LINDBERGH

I am convinced that all writers are optimists whether they concede the point or not... How otherwise could any human being sit down to a pile of blank sheets and decide to write, say two hundred thousand words on a given theme?

THOMAS COSTAIN

If we had to say what writing is, we would define it essentially as an act of courage.

CYNTHIA OZICK

Whatever our theme in writing, it is old and tried. Whatever our place, it has been visited by the stranger, it will never be new again. It is only the vision that can be new; but that is enough.

EUDORA WELTY

The writer, like the priest, must be exempted from secular labor. His work needs a frolic health; he must be at the top of his condition.

RALPH WALDO EMERSON

The writer has taken unto himself the former function of the priest or prophet. He presumes to order and legislate the people's life. There is no person more arrogant than the writer.

CORNELIUS REGISTER

Read, read, read. Read everything—trash, classics, good and bad, and see how they do it. Just like a carpenter who works as an apprentice and studies the master. Read! You'll absorb it. Then write. If it is good, you'll find out. If it's not, throw it out the window.

WILLIAM FAULKNER

If you're a singer, you lose your voice. A baseball player loses his arm. A writer gets more knowledge, and if he's good, the older he gets, the better he writes.

MICKEY SPILLANE

It took me fifteen years to discover I had no talent for writing, but I couldn't give it up because by that time I was too famous.

ROBERT BENCHLEY

Success comes to a writer, as a rule, so gradually that it is always something of a shock to him to look back and realize the heights to which he has climbed.

P. G. WODEHOUSE

A writer has nothing to say after the age of forty; if he is clever he knows how to hide it.

GEORGES SIMENON

We're not professional athletes; it's reasonable to assume that we'll get better as we mature—at least, until we start getting senile. Of course, some writers who write their best books early simply lose their interest in writing; or they lose their concentration— probably because they want to do other things.

JOHN IRVING

You must not suppose, because I am a man of letters, that I never tried to earn an honest living.

GEORGE BERNARD SHAW

An incurable itch for scribbling takes possession of many and grows inveterate in their insane hearts.

JUVENAL

A writer is somebody for whom writing is more difficult than it is for other people.

THOMAS MANN

Another damned thick, square book! Always scribble, scribble! Eh! Mr. Gibbon?

> THE DUKE OF GLOUCESTER, upon accepting the second volume of A *History of the Decline and Fall of the Roman Empire* from its author.

When you get to the footnote at the bottom of the page, like as not all you find is *ibid. Ibid* is a great favorite of footnote-mad authors. It was a great favorite of Gibbon. How come fiction writers do not need footnotes?

> FRANK SULLIVAN

The devoted writer of humor must continue to try to come as close to the truth as he can, even if he gets burned in the process, but I don't think he will get too badly burned. His faith in the good will, the soundness, and the sense of humor of his countrymen will always serve as his asbestos curtain.

> JAMES THURBER

It's much easier to write a solemn book than a funny book. It's harder to make people laugh than it is to make them cry. People are always on the verge of tears.

> FRAN LEBOWITZ

I don't drink a lot. That's perhaps one of the reasons why my characters are always drinking and taking drugs, because I am not.
ROBERT STONE

Boozing does not necessarily have to go hand in hand with being a writer, as seems to be the concept in America. I therefore solemnly declare to all young men trying to become writers that they do not actually have to become drunkards first.
NELSON ALDRICH

I like to stay up late at night and get drunk and sleep late. I wish I could break the habit but I can't. The afternoon is the only time I have left and I try to use it to the best advantage, with a hangover.
WILLIAM STYRON

Some American writers who have known each other for years have never met in the daytime or when both were sober.
JAMES THURBER

I usually need a can of beer to prime me.
NORMAN MAILER

No one, ever, wrote anything as well even after one drink as he would have done without it.
RING LARDNER

I wrote a short story because I wanted to see something of mine in print other than my fingers.

WILSON MIZNER

I put a piece of paper under my pillow, and when I could not sleep I wrote in the dark.

HENRY DAVID THOREAU

I put things down on sheets of paper and stuff them in my pockets. When I have enough, I have a book.

JOHN LENNON

Failure is very difficult for a writer to bear, but very few can manage the shock of early success.

MAURICE VALENCY

It was extraordinary but because all that time I was a failure, I knew it was a mistake. I should have gone out into the world of periodicals and journalism. Publish, publish whatever you can as early as possible. Not to be published as a novelist until you are 37 years old is devastating, a kind of living death. I'll never get over it. It has left me with almost an excess of gratitude for any attention I get.

CYNTHIA OZICK

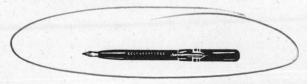

This is what I find encouraging about the writing trades: They allow mediocre people who are patient and industrious to revise their stupidity, to edit themselves into something like intelligence. They also allow lunatics to seem saner than sane.

KURT VONNEGUT, JR.

Some men borrow books; some men steal books; and others beg presentation copies from the author.

JAMES JEFFREY ROCHE

From the moment I picked your book up until I laid it down I was convulsed with laughter. Someday I intend reading it.

GROUCHO MARX, on S. J. Perelman's first book

It is the part of prudence to thank an author for his book before reading it, so as to avoid the necessity of lying about it afterwards.

GEORGE SANTAYANA

No one can write decently who is distrustful of the reader's intelligence, or whose attitude is patronizing.

E. B. WHITE

They always think that if you write well you're somehow cheating, you're not being democratic by writing as badly as everybody else does.

GORE VIDAL

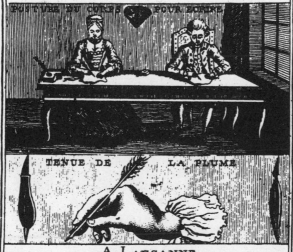

People do not deserve to have good writing, they are so pleased with bad.

RALPH WALDO EMERSON

If you want to get rich from writing, write the sort of thing that's read by persons who move their lips when they're reading to themselves.

DON MARQUIS

In my opinion the readers of novels are far more intelligent than unsuccessful writers will believe. They are expert in detecting and merciless to the conceited author, and the insincere author, and the author with all the tools of literature at his command who has nothing to say worth reading.

NEVIL SHUTE

Nature, not content with denying him the ability to think, has endowed him with the ability to write.

A. E. HOUSMAN

If I could think, maybe I wouldn't write.

SCOTT SPENCER

Writing is an adventure. To begin with, it is a toy and an amusement. Then it becomes a mistress, then it becomes a master, then it becomes a tyrant. The last phase is that just as you are about to be reconciled to your servitude, you kill the monster and fling him to the public.

WINSTON CHURCHILL

Writing is the hardest work in the world not involving heavy lifting.

PETER HAMILL

Writing is manual labor of the mind: a job, like laying pipe.

JOHN GREGORY DUNNE

Writing is like walking in a deserted street. Out of the dust in the street you make a mud pie.

JOHN LE CARRE

When a book, any sort of book, reaches a certain intensity of artistic performance it becomes literature. Than intensity may be a matter of style, situation, character, emotional tone, or idea, or half a dozen other things. It may also be a perfection of control over the movement of a story similar to the control a great pitcher has over a ball.

RAYMOND CHANDLER

Literature is an occupation in which you have to keep proving your talent to people who have none.

JULES RENARD

To write weekly, to write daily, to write shortly, to write for busy people catching trains in the morning or for tired people coming home in the evening, is a heartbreaking task for men who know good writing from bad.

VIRGINIA WOOLF

The art of newspaper paragraphing is to stroke a platitude until it purrs like an epigram.

DON MARQUIS

A journalist is a grumbler, a censurer, a giver of advice, a regent of sovereigns, a tutor of nations. Four hostile newspapers are more to be feared than a thousand bayonets.

NAPOLEON BONAPARTE

The difference between journalism and literature is that journalism is unreadable and literature is not read.

OSCAR WILDE

The first thing an unpublished author should remember is that no one asked him to write in the first place. With this firmly in mind, he has no right to become discouraged just because other people are being published.

JOHN FARRAR

Literature is news that STAYS news.

EZRA POUND

Writing is so difficult that I often feel that writers, having had their hell on earth, will escape all punishment hereafter.

JESSAMYN WEST

When I hear about writer's block, this one and that one! f**k off! Stop writing, for Christ's sake: Plenty more where you came from.

GORE VIDAL

You can always write something. You write limericks. You write a love letter. You do something to get you in the habit of writing again, to bring back the desire.

ERSKINE CALDWELL

I think I did pretty well, considering I started out with nothing but a bunch of blank paper.

STEVE MARTIN

My two fingers on a typewriter have never connected with my brain. My hand on a pen does. A fountain pen, of course. Ball-point pens are only good for filling out forms on a plane.

GRAHAM GREENE

If the first novel is successful, the writer buys a serious, writerly object that bespeaks investment and confidence—a word processor, a new bookshelf, reams of white paper. . . . In any case, a new and bigger wastebasket.

JAYNE ANNE PHILLIPS

The machine has several virtues. . . . One may lean back in his chair and work it. It piles an awful stack of words on one page. It don't muss things or scatter ink blots around.

from MARK TWAIN'S first letter written on a typewriter

What is a writer but a schmuck with an Underwood?

JACK WARNER

Sometimes I think it sounds like I walked out of the room and left the typewriter running.

GENE FOWLER

I just sit at a typewriter and curse it a bit.

P. G. WODEHOUSE

There exists an inverse correlation between the size of a ball and the quality of writing about the sport in which the ball is used. There are superb books about golf, very good books about baseball, not very good books about football, few good books about basketball, and no good books about beachballs.

GEORGE PLIMPTON

Poets are like baseball pitchers. Both have their moments. The intervals are the tough things.

ROBERT FROST

They can't yank a novelist like they can a pitcher. A novelist has to go the full nine, even if it kills him.

ERNEST HEMINGWAY

We romantic writers are there to make people feel and not think. A historical romance is the only kind of book where chastity really counts.

BARBARA CARTLAND

To read a group of novels these days is a depressing experience. After the fourth or fifth, I find myself thinking about 'The Novel' and I feel a desperate desire to sneak out to a movie.

LESLIE FIEDLER

When I was a boy, people were already talking about fiction going downhill. In the years that have elapsed, almost everything has gone downhill, including the people who said it. But fiction remains at the top of the tree.

SIR OSBERT SITWELL

I think you must remember that a writer is a simple-minded person to begin with and go on that basis. He's not a great mind, he's not a great thinker, he's not a great philosopher, he's a storyteller.

ERSKINE CALDWELL

Adam was the only man who, when he said a good thing, knew that nobody had said it before him.

MARK TWAIN

Immature artists imitate. Mature artists steal.
LIONEL TRILLING

Good swiping is an art in itself.
JULES FEIFFER

When a thing has been said and well said, have no
scruple; take it and copy it. Give references? Why
should you? Either your readers know where you have
taken the passage and the precaution is needless, or
they do not know and you humiliate them.
ANATOLE FRANCE

Remember why the good Lord made your eyes,
Pla-gi-a-rize!
TOM LEHRER

It has come to be practically a sort of rule in literature, that a man, having once shown himself capable
of original writing, is entitled thenceforth to steal
from the writings of others at discretion.
RALPH WALDO EMERSON

If you copy from one author it's plagiarism. If you
copy from two, it's research.
WILSON MIZNER

If placed in a situation where you must quote another author, always write "[sic]" after any word that may be misspelled or looks the least bit questionable in any way. If there are no misspellings or curious words, toss in a few "[sic]"s just to break up the flow. By doing this, you will appear to be knowledgeable and "on your toes," while the one quoted will seem suspect and vaguely discredited.

MICHAEL O'DONOGHUE

Next o'er his books his eyes began to roll,
In pleasing memory of all he stole.

ALEXANDER POPE

I have made three rules of writing for myself that are absolutes: Never take advice. Never show or discuss work in progress. Never answer a critic.

RAYMOND CHANDLER

Just get it down on paper, and then we'll see what to do with it.

MAXWELL PERKINS' advice to Marcia Davenport

There are three rules for writing the novel. Unfortunately, no one knows what they are.

W. SOMERSET MAUGHAM

Never make excuses, never let them see you bleed, and never get separated from your baggage.

from WESLEY PRICE'S *Three Rules of Professional Comportment for Writers*

The most valuable writing habit I have is not to answer questions about my writing habits.

CHRISTOPHER MORLEY

Writing is for the most part a lonely and unsatisfying occupation. One is tied to a table, a chair, a stack of paper.

GRAHAM GREENE

I write when I'm inspired, and I see to it that I'm inspired at nine o'clock every morning.

PETER DE VRIES

When I am working on a book or a story I write every morning as soon after the first light as possible. There is no one to disturb you and it is cool or cold and you come to your work and warm as you write.

ERNEST HEMINGWAY

I generally go to work right after breakfast. I sit right down to the machine. If I find I'm not able to write, I quit.

HENRY MILLER

You can do it sitting down. I sit in bed with a big breakfast and then I write. I like that.
KATHARINE HEPBURN

I work every day, from ten in the morning till I'm done with my pages. I try not to write beyond a certain point. It's my experience that if I write too much in one day it kills a couple of days' work for me after that. I like to keep myself to three or four pages a day.
SCOTT SPENCER

Three hours a day will produce as much as a man ought to write.
ANTHONY TROLLOPE

The tools I need for my work are paper, tobacco, food, and a little whiskey.
WILLIAM FAULKNER

I type in one place, but I write all over the house.
TONI MORRISON

The ideal view for daily writing, hour on hour, is the blank brick wall of a cold-storage warehouse. Failing this, a stretch of sky will do, cloudless if possible.
EDNA FERBER

What I adore is supreme professionalism. I'm bored by writers who can write only when it is raining.
NOEL COWARD

Writing is a wholetime job: no professional writer can afford only to write when he feels like it.

W. SOMERSET MAUGHAM

You write by sitting down and writing. There's no particular time or place—you suit yourself, your nature. How one works, assuming he's disciplined, doesn't matter.

BERNARD MALAMUD

I'm not a big believer in disciplined writers. What does discipline mean? The writer who forces himself to sit down and write for seven hours every day might be wasting those seven hours if he's not in the mood and doesn't feel the juice. I don't think discipline equals creativity.

BRET EASTON ELLIS

The perfect place for a writer is in the hideous roar of a city, with men making a new road under his window in competition with a barrel organ, and on the mat a man waiting for the rent.

HENRY VOLLAM MORTON

When I have trouble writing. I step outside my studio into the garden and pull weeds until my mind clears— I find weeding to be the best therapy there is for writer's block.

IRVING STONE

Everything goes by the board: humor, pride, decency. . . . to get the book written. If a writer has to rob his mother, he will not hesitate; the *Ode on a Grecian Urn* is worth any number of old ladies.

WILLIAM FAULKNER

Writing is a solitary occupation. Family, friends, and society are the natural enemies of a writer. He must be alone, uninterrupted, and slightly savage if he is to sustain and complete an undertaking.

LAWRENCE CLARK POWELL

Writing is an escape from a world that crowds me. I like being alone in a room. It's almost a form of meditation—an investigation of my own life. It has nothing to do with "I've got to get another play."

NEIL SIMON

If you're trying to write, you have to let your attention drop. You can't maintain an interest in anything else.

BARBARA TUCHMAN

It sounds shameful, but on my best days I write only about three or four hours.

ANNE BERNAYS

There comes a moment in the day, when you have written your pages in the morning, attended to your correspondence in the afternoon, and have nothing further to do. Then comes the hour when you are bored; that's the time for sex.

H. G. WELLS

I felt like you can write forever, but you have a short time to raise a family. And I think a family is a lot more important than writing.

KEN KESEY

All my major works have been written is prison. . . . I would recommend prison not only to aspiring writers but to aspiring politicians, too.

JAWAHARLAL NEHRU

You have to sink way down to a level of hopelessness and desperation to find the book that you can write.

SUSAN SONTAG

The best time for planning a book is while you're do-ing the dishes.

AGATHA CHRISTIE

What no wife of a writer can ever understand is that a writer is working when he's staring out of the window.

BURTON RASCOE

Often while reading a book one feels that the author would have preferred to paint rather than write; one can sense the pleasure he derives from describing a landscape or a person, as if he were painting what he is saying, because deep in his heart he would have preferred to use brushes and colors.

PABLO PICASSO

Writing is a form of therapy; sometimes I wonder how all those who do not write, compose or paint can manage to escape the madness, the melancholia, the panic fear which is inherent in a human situation.

GRAHAM GREENE

It's a nervous work. The state that you need to write in is the state that others are paying large sums to get rid of.

SHIRLEY HAZZARD

The man of letters loves not only to be read but to be seen. Happy to be by himself, he would be happier still if people knew that he was happy to be by himself, working in solitude at night under his lamp.

REMY DE GOURMONT

If I could I would always work in silence and obscurity, and let my efforts be known by their results.

EMILY BRONTE

Only ambitious nonentities and hearty mediocrities exhibit their rough drafts. It is like passing around samples of one's sputum.

VLADIMIR NABOKOV

It makes me so uncomfortable for them. If they're talking about a plot idea, I feel the idea is probably going to evaporate. I want to almost physically reach over and cover their mouths and say, 'You'll lose it if you're not careful.'

ANNE TYLER

I just think it's bad to talk about one's present work, for it spoils something at the root of the creative act. It discharges the tension.

NORMAN MAILER

Mostly, we authors must repeat ourselves—that's the truth. We have two or three great moving experiences in our lives—experiences so great and moving that it doesn't seem at the time that anyone else has been caught up and pounded and dazzled and astonished and beaten and broken and rescued and illuminated and rewarded and humbled in just that way ever before.

F. SCOTT FITZGERALD

I think that in order to write really well and convincingly, one must be somewhat poisoned by emotion. Dislike, displeasure, resentment, fault-finding, imagination, passionate remonstrance, a sense of injustice—they all make fine fuel.

EDNA FERBER

What I find is that I can write *and* do other things. When the creative urge seizes one—at, least, such is my experience—one becomes creative in all directions at once.

HENRY MILLER

I wrote the scenes . . . by using the same apprehensive imagination that occurs in the morning before an afternoon's appointment with my dentist.

JOHN MARQUAND

I've always believed in writing without a collaborator, because where two people are writing the same book, each believes he gets all the worries and only half the royalties.

AGATHA CHRISTIE

You can fire your secretary, divorce your spouse, abandon your children. But they remain your co-authors forever.

ELLEN GOODMAN

I never could understand how two men can write a book together; to me that's like three people getting together to have a baby.

EVELYN WAUGH

To be an illustrator is to be a participant. Someone who has something equally important to offer as the writer of the book—occasionally something more important—but is certainly never the writer's echo.

MAURICE SENDAK

Why do people always expect authors to answer questions? I am an author because I want to ask questions. If I had answers I'd be a politician.

EUGENE IONESCO

INTERVIEWER: How many drafts of a story do you do?

S. J. PERELMAN: Thirty-seven. I once tried doing thirty-three, but something was lacking, a certain—how shall I say?—je ne sais quoi. On another occasion, I tried forty-two versions, but the final effect was too lapidary—you know what I mean, Jack? What the hell are you trying to extort—my trade secrets?

People who read me seem to be divided into four groups: twenty-five percent like me for the right reasons; twenty-five percent like me for the wrong reason; twenty-five percent hate me for the right reasons. It's that last twenty-five percent that worries me.

ROBERT FROST

An author ought to write for the youth of his own generation, the critics of the next, and the schoolmasters of ever afterwards.

F. SCOTT FITZGERALD

When I want to read a good book, I write one.

BENJAMIN DISRAELI

I can't understand why a person will take a year to write a novel when he can easily buy one for a few dollars.

FRED ALLEN

I never desire to converse with a man who has written more than he has read.

SAMUEL JOHNSON

I only read two books in my life and that includes The Official Pete Rose Scrapbook. That's not a book—that's a bunch of pictures. I done the captions. I've written more damn books than I've read.

PETE ROSE

Only when one has lost all curiosity about the future has one reached the age to write an autobiography.

EVELYN WAUGH

And because I found I had nothing else to write about, I presented myself as a subject.

MONTAIGNE

I often quote myself. It adds spice to my conversation.

GEORGE BERNARD SHAW

Let it be kept until the ninth year, the manuscript put away at home: you may destroy whatever you haven't published; once out, what you've said can't be stopped.

HORACE

I'll be eighty this month. Age, if nothing else, entitles me to set the record straight before I dissolve. I've given my memoirs far more thought than any of my marriages. You can't divorce a book.

GLORIA SWANSON

A well-written life is almost as rare as a well-spent one.

THOMAS CARLYLE

The man who writes about himself and his own time is the only man who writes about all people and about all time.

GEORGE BERNARD SHAW

How can one make a life out of six cardboard boxes full of tailors' bills, love letters and old picture post-cards?

VIRGINIA WOOLF

When you see that many letters and that many documents and gotten that far into the situation, you are likely to start seeing your subject as a relative.

LEON EDEL, on biographers

When you read a biography, remember that the truth is never fit for publication.

GEORGE BERNARD SHAW

On the trail of another man, the biographer must put up with finding himself at every turn: any biography uneasily shelters an autobiography within it.

PAUL MURRAY KENDALL

Biographers want to appropriate something from their subjects. There is something their subjects have that they want.

PHYLLIS ROSP

A novelist, in his omniscience, knows the measure of his characters, out of his passion for all sorts of conditions of human life. The biographer, however, begins with certain limiting little facts.

LEON EDEL

The novel is the highest example of subtle interrelatedness that man has discovered.

D. H. LAWRENCE

Reading about imaginary characters and their adventures is the greatest pleasure in the world. Or the second greatest.

ANTHONY BURGESS

As a fiction writer I find it convenient not to believe things. Not to disbelieve them either, just move them into a realm where everything is held in suspension.

WILLIAM GASS

I did not begin to write novels until I had forgotten all I had learned at school and college.

JOHN GALSWORTHY

All of us learn to write in the second grade. Most of us then go on to greater things.

basketball coach BOBBY KNIGHT

What makes a good writer of history is a guy who is suspicious. Suspicion marks the real difference between the man who wants to write honest history and the one who'd rather write a good story.

JIM BISHOP

People need books with an epic background. They are bored with books that tell only one story on one level. They need something fantastic, something that gives them a sense of living in history. As it is, most novels aren't giving readers a chance to use their sense of history.

GUNTER GRASS

Everyone who works in the domain of fiction is a bit crazy. The problem is to render this craziness interesting.

FRANCOIS TRUFFAUT

Every author really wants to have letters printed in the papers. Unable to make the grade, he drops down a rung of the ladder and writes novels.

P. G. WODEHOUSE

One of the dumbest things you were ever taught was to write what you know. Because what you know is usually dull. Remember when you first wanted to be a writer? Eight or 10 years old, reading about thin-lipped heroes flying over mysterious viny jungles toward untold wonders? That's what you wanted to write about, about what you didn't know.

KEN KESEY

I have never met an author who admitted that people did not buy his book because it was dull.

W. SOMERSET MAUGHAM

Prose books are the show dogs I breed and sell to support my cat.

> ROBERT GRAVES, on writing novels to support his love of writing poetry.

Writing is a dog's life, but the only life worth living.

> GUSTAVE FLAUBERT

The value of great fiction, we begin to suspect, is not that it entertains us or distracts us from our troubles, not just that it broadens our knowledge of people and places, but also that it helps us to know what we believe, reinforces the qualities that are noblest in us, leads us to feel uneasy about our failures and limitations.

> JOHN GARDNER

When audiences come to see us authors lecture, it is largely in the hope that we'll be funnier to look at than to read.

> SINCLAIR LEWIS

A writer's problem does not change. He himself changes and the world he lives in changes, but his problem remains the same. It is always how to write truly and, having found out what is true, to project it in such a way that it becomes a part of the experience of the person who reads it.

> ERNEST HEMINGWAY

A writer is congenitally unable to tell the truth and that is why we call what he writes fiction.

WILLIAM FAULKNER

How pleasant it is to respect people! When I see books, I am not concerned with how the authors loved or played cards; I see only their marvellous works.

ANTON CHEKHOV

Getting even is one reason for writing.

WILLIAM GASS

Writers seldom choose as friends those self-contained characters who are never in trouble, never unhappy or ill, never make mistakes, and always count their change when it is handed to them.

CATHERINE DRINKER BOWEN

There is only one trait that marks the writer. He is always watching. It's a kind of trick of the mind and he is born with it.

MORLEY CALLAGHAN

When you're a writer, you no longer see things with the freshness of the normal person. There are always two figures that work inside you, and if you are at all intelligent you realize that you have lost something. But I think there has always been this dichotomy in a real writer. He wants to be terribly human, and he responds emotionally, and at the same time there's this cold observer who cannot cry.

BRIAN MOORE

No tears in the writer, no tears in the reader. No surprise for the writer, no surprise for the reader.

ROBERT FROST

How can you write if you can't cry?

RING LARDNER

The novelist who refuses sentiment refuses the full spectrum of human behavior, and then he just dries up. Irony is always scratching your tired ass, whatever way you look at it. I would rather give full vent to all human loves and disappointments, and take a chance on being corny, than die a smartass.

JIM HARRISON

In any work that is truly creative, I believe, the writer cannot be omniscient in advance about the effects that he proposes to produce. The suspense of a novel is not only in the reader, but in the novelist, who is intensely curious about what will happen to the hero.

MARY MC CARTHY

Writing a book is a horrible, exhausting struggle, like a long bout of some painful illness. One would never undertake such a thing if one were not driven by some demon whom one can neither resist nor understand. For all one knows that demon is simply the same instinct that makes a baby squall for attention. And yet it is also true that one can write nothing readable unless one constantly struggles to efface one's personality. Good prose is like a windowpane.

GEORGE ORWELL

They're fancy talkers about themselves, writers. If I had to give young writers advice, I would say don't listen to writers talk about themselves.

LILLIAN HELLMAN

Advice to young writers? Always the same advice: learn to trust your own judgement, learn inner independence, learn to trust that time will sort the good from the bad—including your own bad.

DORIS LESSING

My point to young writers is to socialize. Don't just go up to a pine cabin all alone and brood. You reach that stage soon enough anyway.

CYRIL CONNOLLY

Most writers, you know, are awful sticks to talk with.

SHERWOOD ANDERSON

All writers are vain, selfish, and lazy, and at the very
bottom of their motives there lies a mystery.

GEORGE ORWELL

Writers seldom wish other writers well.

SAUL BELLOW

What a heartbreaking job it is trying to combine authors for their own protection! I had ten years of it on
the Committee of Management of the Society of Authors; and the first lesson I learned was that when you
take the field for the authors you will be safer without
a breastplate than without a backplate.

GEORGE BERNARD SHAW

If I didn't know the ending of a story, I wouldn't begin. I always write my last line, my last paragraph, my
last page first.

KATHERINE ANNE PORTER

I always know the ending; that's where I start.

TONI MORRISON

The persistent problem with my writing is that I never
know how something is going to come out; even when
I write a short review, I always have to start over. I
have no mastery. But it's actually beneficial—it pre-
vents things from becoming routine.

HEINRICH BOLL

Writing every book is like a purge; at the end of it one is empty . . . like a dry shell on the beach, waiting for the tide to come in again.

DAPHNE DU MAURIER

Writing everyday is a way of keeping the engine running, and then something good may come out of it.

T. S. ELIOT

We need not worry much about writers. Man will always find a means to gratify a passion. He will write, as he commits adultery, in spite of taxation.

GRAHAM GREENE

I can always find plenty of women to sleep with but the kind of woman that is really hard for me to find is a typist who can read my writing.

THOMAS WOLFE

One hates an author that's all author.

LORD BYRON

Your manuscript is both good and original; but the part that is good is not original, and the part that is original is not good.

SAMUEL JOHNSON

Whenever you feel an impulse to perpetrate a piece of exceptionally fine writing, obey it . . . and delete it before sending your manuscript to the press.

SIR ARTHUR QUILLER-COUCH

Manuscript: something submitted in haste and returned at leisure.

OLIVER HERFORD

I discovered that rejections are not altogether a bad thing. They teach a writer to rely on his own judgment and to say in his heart of hearts, "To hell with you."

SAUL BELLOW

A good many young writers make the mistake of enclosing a stamped, self-addressed envelope, big enough for the manuscript to come back in. This is too much of a temptation for the editor.

RING LARDNER

I've never signed a contract, so never have a deadline. A deadline's an unnerving thing. I just finish a book, and if the publisher doesn't like it that's his privilege. There've been many, many rejections. If you want to write it your own way, that's the chance you take.

MARCHETTE CHUTE

Most serious writers work slowly and, thus, miss deadlines, sometimes several deadlines, publishers' deadlines, that is. A serious writer cannot have any deadline but his own.

MERLE MILLER

They didn't want it good, they wanted it Wednesday.
ROBERT HEINLEIN

Never submit an idea or chapter to an editor or publisher, no matter how much he would like you to. Writing from the approved idea is (another) gravely serious time-waster. This is your story. Try and find out what your editor wants in advance, but then try and give it to him in one piece.
JOHN CREASEY

We have read your manuscript with boundless delight. If we were to publish your paper, it would be impossible for us to publish any work of lower standard. And as it is unthinkable that in the next thousand years we shall see its equal, we are, to our regret, compelled to return your divine composition, and to beg you a thousand times to overlook our short sight and timidity.

Rejection slip from a Chinese economic journal, quoted in the *Financial Times*.

Only a small minority of authors over-write themselves. Most of the good and the tolerable ones do not write enough.
ARNOLD BENNETT

There are only two ways in which a writer can become important—to write a great deal, and have his writings appear everywhere, or to write very little. It is a question of temperament.

J. H. WOODS

The faster I write the better my output. If I'm going slow I'm in trouble. It means I'm pushing the words instead of being pulled by them.

RAYMOND CHANDLER

With sixty staring me in the face I have developed inflammation of the sentence structure and a definite hardening of the paragraphs.

JAMES THURBER, at age 59.

A collection of short stories is generally thought to be a horrendous clinker; an enforced courtesy for the elderly writer who wants to display the trophies of his youth, along with his trout flies.

JOHN CHEEVER

I finished my first book seventy-six years ago. I offered it to every publisher on the English-speaking earth I had ever heard of. Their refusals were unanimous: and it did not get into print until, fifty years later, publishers would publish anything that had my name of it.

GEORGE BERNARD SHAW

Literary success of any enduring kind is made by refusing to do what publishers want, by refusing to
write what the public wants, by refusing to accept any
popular standard, by refusing to write anything to
order.

LAFCADIO HEARN

A book must be done according to the writer's con-
ception of it as nearly perfect as possible, and the
publishing problems begin then. That is, the publisher
must not try to get a writer to fit the book to the conditions of the trade, etc. It must be the other way
around.

MAXWELL PERKINS

In the march up the heights of fame there comes a
spot close to the summit in which man reads nothing
but detective stories.

HEYWOOD HALE BROUN

At least half the mystery novels published violate the
law that the solution, once revealed, must seem to be
inevitable.

RAYMOND CHANDLER

The beginner who submits a detective novel longer
than 80,000 words is courting rejection.

HOWARD HAYCRAFT

The detective himself should never turn out to be the culprit.

S. S. VAN DINE

Love interest nearly always weakens a mystery because it introduces a type of suspense that is antagonistic to the detective's struggle to solve a problem.

RAYMOND CHANDLER

There has to be a woman, but not much of one. A good horse is much more important.

MAX BRAND, on writing Westerns

The mystery story is two stories in one: the story of what happened and the story of what appeared to happen.

MARY ROBERTS RINEHART

All you need to write a ghost story is put a ghost in it. For a detective story you need a plot.

P. D. JAMES

I think a little menace is fine to have in a story. For one thing, it's good for the circulation.

RAYMOND CARVER

There certainly does seem a possibility that the detective story will come to an end, simply because the public will have learnt all the tricks.

DOROTHY SAYERS

Science fiction stories are whatever science fiction editors buy.

JOHN CAMPBELL

A good science fiction story is a story with a human problem, and a human solution, which would not have happened without its science content.

THEODORE STURGEON

I love you sons of bitches. You're the only ones with guts enough to really care about the future, who really notice what machines do to us, what wars do to us, what cities do to us, what tremendous misunderstanding, mistakes, accidents, and catastrophes do to us. You're the only ones zany enough to agonize over time and distance without limit, over the fact that we are right now determining whether the space voyage for the next billion years or so is going to be Heaven or Hell.

The drunken hero of KURT VONNEGUT's *God Bless You, Mr. Rosewater,* who blunders into a convention of science fiction writers

You don't have to suffer to be a poet. Adolescence is enough suffering for anyone.

JOHN CIARDI

The poet, as everyone knows, must strike his individual note sometime between the ages of fifteen and twenty-five. He may hold it a long time, or a short time, but it is then he must strike it or never. School and college have been conducted with the almost express purpose of keeping him busy with something else till the danger of his ever creating anything has passed.

ROBERT FROST

Prose, poetry, I never separated them. But in your first notebook stage you tend toward poetry, because it's easier at that age. I tried to write prose, but I was never good at the short story.

JIM HARRISON

The crown of literature is poetry. It is its end and aim. It is the sublimest activity of the human mind. It is the achievement of beauty and delicacy. The writer of prose can only step aside when the poet passes.

W. SOMERSET MAUGHAM

Everybody has their own idea of what's a poet. Robert Frost, President Johnson, T. S. Eliot, Rudolf Valentino—they're all poets. I like to think of myself as the one who carries the light bulb.

BOB DYLAN

When power leads man to arrogance, poetry reminds
him of his limitations. When power narrows the area
of man's concern, poetry reminds him of the richness
and diversity of his existence. When power corrupts,
poetry cleanses.

PRESIDENT JOHN KENNEDY, October 26,
1963 at the dedication of the Robert Frost
Library, Amherst College

Women have always been poor, not for two hundred
years merely, but from the beginning of time...
Women, then, have not had a dog's chance of writing
poetry. That is why I have laid so much stress on
money and a room of one's own.

VIRGINIA WOOLF

Modern poets talk against business, poor things, but
all of us write for money. Beginners are subjected to
trial by market, poor things.

ROBERT FROST

Poets are born, not paid.

WILSON MIZNER

Poets aren't very useful.
Because they aren't consumeful or very produceful.

OGDEN NASH

Like a piece of ice on a hot stove the poem must ride
on its own melting.

ROBERT FROST

. GOLD AND SILVER PENCILS. (Hall Marked.)

Publishing a volume of verse is like dropping a rose-petal down the Grand Canyon and waiting for the echo.

DON MARQUIS

Not gods, nor men, nor even booksellers have put up with poets being second-rate.

HORACE

I've had it with these cheap sons of bitches who claim they love poetry but never buy a book.

KENNETH REXROTH

Modesty is a virtue not often found among poets, for almost every one of them thinks himself the greatest in the world.

MIGUEL DE CERVANTES

It's silly to suggest the writing of poetry as something ethereal, a sort of soul-crashing emotional experience that wrings you. I have no fancy ideas about poetry. It doesn't come to you on the wings of a dove. It's something you work hard at.

LOUISE BOGAN

I'd rather be a great bad poet than a good bad poet.

OGDEN NASH

It is always hard for poets to believe that one says their poems are bad not because one is a fiend but because their poems are bad.

RANDALL JARRELL

Poetry is the opening and closing of a door, leaving those who look through to guess about what was seen during a moment.

CARL SANDBURG

Great poetry is always written by somebody straining to go beyond what he can do.

STEPHEN SPENDER

I went for years not finishing anything. Because, of course, when you finish something you can be judged ... I had poems which were re-written so many times I suspect it was just a way of avoiding sending them out.

ERICA JONG

A poem is never a put-up job so to speak. It begins as a lump in the throat, a sense of wrong, a home-sickness, a love sickness. It is never a thought to begin with.

ROBERT FROST

To have written one good poem—good used seriously—is an unlikely and marvellous thing that only a couple hundred of writers of English, at the most, have done—it's like sitting out in the yard in the evening and having a meteorite fall in one's lap.

RANDALL JARRELL

If I feel physically as if the top of my head were taken off, I know that is poetry.
EMILY DICKINSON

A poet's mission is to make others confound fiction and reality in order to render them, for an hour, mysteriously happy.
ISAK DINESON

My quarrel with poets is not that they are unclear, but that they are too diligent.
E. B. WHITE

I was too slow a mover. It was much easier to be a poet.
T. S. ELIOT, on giving up boxing in college

I could no more define poetry than a terrier can define a rat.
A. E. HOUSMAN

No poet, no artist of any art has his complete meaning alone. His significance, his appreciation is the appreciation of his relation to the dead poets and artists. You cannot value him alone; you must set him, for contrast and comparison, among the dead. I mean this as a principle of aesthetic, not merely historical, criticism.
T. S. ELIOT

I believe that every English poet should read the English classics, master the rules of grammar before he attempts to bend or break them, travel abroad, experience the horrors of sordid passion, and—if he is lucky enough—know the love of an honest woman.

ROBERT GRAVES

Were poets to be suppressed, my friends, with no history, no ancient lays, save that each had a father, nothing of any man would be heard hereafter.

GIOLLA BRIGHDE MHAC CON MIDH (circa 1259)

There are three things, after all, that a poem must reach: the eye, the ear, and what we may call the heart or the mind. It is most important of all to reach the heart of the reader.

ROBERT FROST

A good writer is not, per se, a good book critic. No more than a good drunk is automatically a good bartender.

JIM BISHOP

I regard reviews as a kind of infant's disease to which newborn books are subject.

GEORG CHRISTOPH LICHTENBERG

A unanimous chorus of approval is not an assurance of survival; authors who please everyone at once are quickly exhausted.

ANDRE GIDE

The only reason I didn't kill myself after I read the reviews of my first book was because we have two rivers in New York and I couldn't decide which one to jump into.

WILFRID SHEED

One thing I learned about my first novel was what all the reviewers thought of it, from Little Rock to Broken Hill, for I subscribed to a press-cutting agency, a thing I have not done since. I learned thus, what I have had no occasion to unlearn, that reviewers do not read books with much care, and that their profession is more given to stupidity and malice and literary ignorance even than the profession of novelist.

ANTHONY BURGESS

Insects sting, not in malice, but because they want to live. It is the same with critics; they desire our blood, not our pain.

FRIEDRICH NIETZSCHE

Asking a working writer what he thinks about critics is like asking a lamppost what it feels about dogs.

JOHN OSBOURNE

It's surprising that authors should expect kindness to be shown to their books when they are not themselves known for kindness toward their characters, their culture or by implication their readers.

ANATOLE BROYARD

A perfect judge will read each work of wit
With the same spirit that its author writ.

ALEXANDER POPE

Actors yearn for the perfect director, athletes for the perfect coach, priests for the perfect pope, Presidents for the perfect historian. Writers hunger for the perfect reviewer. But this is an imperfect world.

THOMAS FLEMING

Some reviews give pain. That is regrettable, but no author has the right to whine. He was not obliged to be an author. He invited publicity, and he must take the publicity that comes along.

E. M. FORSTER

It is advantageous to an author that his book should be attacked as well as praised. Fame is a shuttlecock. If it be struck at only one end of the room, it will soon fall to the ground. To keep it up, it must be struck at both ends.

SAMUEL JOHNSON

Nothing induces me to read a novel except when I have to make money by writing about it. I detest them.

VIRGINIA WOOLF

Nature fits all her children with something to do;
He who would write and can't write, can surely review.

JAMES RUSSELL LOWELL

It is as hard to find a neutral critic as it is a neutral country in time of war. I suppose if a critic were neutral, he wouldn't trouble to write anything.

KATHERINE ANNE PORTER

A serious reviewer should have an axe to grind. If you don't, your judgements will appear ephemeral, casual, even indifferent. But when you have an axe to grind, it is essential that you should not know what it is, and neither should anyone else.

ANATOLE BROYARD

I am sitting in the smallest room in my house. I have your review in front of me. Soon it will be behind me.

German composer MAX REGER

"Was it Eliot's toilet I saw?"
Palindrome allegedly uttered by an American publisher after paying his first visit to the London firm of Faber and Faber

Whenever I publish a book, I feel like a trapper caught by the Iroquois. They're all lined up with tomahawks, and the idea is to run through with your head down, and everybody gets to take a swing. They hit you in the head, the back, the ass, the balls.

STEPHEN KING

A person who publishes a book willfully appears before the populace with his pants down ... If it is a good book nothing can hurt him. If it is a bad book, nothing can help him.

EDNA ST. VINCENT MILLAY

It is safer to assume that every writer has read every word of every review, and will never forgive you.

JOHN LEONARD

When a man publishes a book, there are so many stupid things said that he declares he'll never do it again. The praise is almost always worse than the criticism.

SHERWOOD ANDERSON

I have long felt that any reviewer who expresses rage and loathing for a novel is preposterous. He or she is like a person who has put on full armor and attacked a hot fudge sundae or a banana split.

KURT VONNEGUT, JR.

Confronted by an absolutely infuriating review it is sometimes helpful for the victim to do a little personal research on the critic. Is there any truth to the rumor that he had no formal education beyond the age of eleven? In any event, is he able to construct a simple English sentence? Do his participles dangle? When moved to lyricism does he write "I had a fun time"? Was he ever arrested for burglary? I don't know that you will prove anything this way, but it is perfectly harmless and quite soothing.

JEAN KERR

Now I feel that dealing with talent is a hazardous occupation. I feel there ought to be some limitation, some qualification of somebody setting up as agent to handle situations like this. The writer isn't supposed to know what's going on. He can only give his attention to one thing.

NELSON ALGREN

An author who gives a manager or publisher any rights in his work except those immediately and specifically required for its publication or performance is for business purposes an imbecile. As 99 per cent of English authors and 100 per cent of American ones are just such imbeciles, managers and publishers make a practice of asking for every right the author possesses.

GEORGE BERNARD SHAW

Let every eye negotiate for itself, and trust no agent.
WILLIAM SHAKESPEARE

I am absolutely convinced that every author of large and varied output ought to put the whole of his affairs into the hands of a good agent, and that every such author who fails to do so loses money by his omission.
ARNOLD BENNETT

In the past I was not so wise as I am now; I left nearly all my business to an agent. I am still encumbered with his slovenly and disadvantageous agreements.
H. G. WELLS

Literature is like any other trade; you will never sell anything unless you go to the right shop.
GEORGE BERNARD SHAW

Writers hop from publisher to publisher mainly because of the size of the dollar, and their loyalty tends to be more toward the agent than either the publisher or editor.
SCOTT MEREDITH

An editor should tell the author his writing is better than it is. Not a lot better, a little better.
T. S. ELIOT

Editors are extremely fallible people, all of them. Don't put too much trust in them.

MAXWELL PERKINS

The job of editor in a publishing house is the dullest, hardest, most exciting, exasperating and rewarding of perhaps any job in the world.

JOHN HALL WHEELOCK

Most editors generally can't recognize bad writing when they read it. Nor do they try very hard to learn to recognize it.

ALFRED KNOPF

Some editors are failed writers, but so are most writers.

T. S. ELIOT

Editing is the same thing as quarreling with writers— same thing exactly.

HAROLD ROSS

Listen carefully to first criticisms of your work. Note just what it is about your work that the critics don't like—then cultivate it. That's the part of your work that's individual and worth keeping.

JEAN COCTEAU

Nine out of ten writers, I am sure, could write more. I think they should and, if they did, they would find their work improving even beyond their own, their agent's and their editor's highest hopes.

JOHN CREASEY

No passion in the world is equal to the passion to alter someone else's draft.

H. G. WELLS

Great editors do not discover nor produce great authors; great authors create and produce great publishers.

JOHN FARRAR

The average editor cannot escape feeling that telling a writer to do something is almost the same thing as performing it himself.

HEYWOOD CAMPBELL BROUN

Writing for the magazines sounds like a delightful occupation, but literally it means nothing without the cooperation of the editors of the magazines, and it is this cooperation which is difficult to secure.

A. A. MILNE

Don't forget, both you and the editor are putting on an unceasing act for the public, and between you there should be the same relation that exists between the magician and his assistant, offstage.

JACK WOODFORD

Editors at work

Never buy an editor or publisher a lunch or a drink until he has bought an article, story or book from you. This rule is absolute and may be broken at your peril.

JOHN CREASEY

It's a damn good story. If you have any comments, write them on the back of a check.

ERLE STANLEY GARDNER, writing to an editor.

Calvin Trillin once proposed that "the advance for a book should be at least as much as the cost of the lunch at which it was discussed." When he asked an editor what he thought of this formula, he was told that it was "unrealistic."

WILLARD ESPY

The writer who can't do his job looks to his editor to do it for him, though he wouldn't dream of offering to share his royalties with that editor.

ALFRED KNOPF

The truth is that editing lines is not necessarily the same as editing a book. A book is a much more complicated entity and totality than the sum of its lines alone. Its structural integrity, the relation and proportions of its parts, and its total impact could escape even a conscientious editor exclusively intent on vetting the book line by line.

BOB GOTTLIEB

I have performed the necessary butchery. Here is the bleeding corpse.

HENRY JAMES, following a request from the TLS to cut three lines from a 5,000 word article.

Everyone needs an editor.

TIM FOOTE, commenting in Time magazine on the fact that Hitler's original title for *Mein Kampf* was *Four-and-a-Half Years of Struggle against Lies, Stupidity, and Cowardice*

You know how it is in the kid's book world: It's just bunny eat bunny.

ANONYMOUS

One should fight like the devil the temptation to think well of editors. They are all, without exception—at least some of the time—incompetent or crazy. By the nature of their profession they read too much, with the result they grow jaded and cannot recognize talent though it dances in front of their eyes.

JOHN GARDNER

An editor should have a pimp for a brother, so he'd have someone to look up to.

GENE FOWLER

It circulated for five years, through the halls of fifteen publishers, and finally ended up with Vanguard Press, which, as you can see, is rather deep into the alphabet.

PATRICK DENNIS, commenting on *Auntie Mame*

Editors are no longer father-confessors. Most of them are acquisition editors who are more concerned with bringing home the bacon than in trying to rewrite the bacon.

SCOTT MEREDITH

There are acquiring editors and line editors. Or you might say line editors and editors with a line. The latter are seen at all the right places. They know just everybody, go everywhere there might be prospective authors: parties, readings, symposia, writers' conferences. The line editor stays at home and edits, line by line. One dredges, the other cleans up.

GARDNER E. LEWIS

A competent editor is a publisher in microcosm, able to initiate and follow a project all the way through.

MARC JAFFE

The one thing I have learned about editing over the years is that you have to edit and publish out of your own tastes, enthusiasms, and concerns, and not out of notions or guesswork about what other people might like to read.

NORMAN COUSINS

Then, in the end, you have your editor go out for himself as the publisher, on the basis of certain resolutions. One of these, is to my mind, a complete betrayal of his profession—that he will only publish books which will coincide with his own views.

MAXWELL PERKINS

You ask for the distinction between the terms "Editor" and "Publisher": an editor selects manuscripts; a publisher selects editors.

MAX SCHUSTER

No, no, there must be a limit to the baseness even of publishers.

DOROTHY SAYERS

Publishers are all cohorts of the devil; there must be a special hell for them somewhere.

GOETHE

As repressed sadists are supposed to become policemen or butchers, so those with irrational fear of life become publishers.

CYRIL CONNOLLY

One of the signs of Napoleon's greatness is the fact that he once had a publisher shot.

SIEGFRIED UNSELF

Gone today, here tomorrow.

ALFRED KNOPF, on book returns

At a London cocktail party, a woman came up to publisher Jonathan Cape and asked, 'Do you keep a copy of every book you print?' He replied, "Madam, I keep thousands."

I do not think publishing at all creditable either to men or women, and (though you will not believe me) very often feel ashamed of it myself.
BYRON, in a letter to Lady Caroline Lamb

I do not think publishing is hard work. I like publishing because it is possible to survive one's mistakes.
MICHAEL JOSEPH

There are men that will make you books and turn 'em loose into the world with as much dispatch as they would do a dish of fritters.
MIGUEL DE CERVANTES

People feel no obligation to buy books, It isn't their fault. Art seems cheap to them, because almost always it is cheap. . . . People stick any kind of stuff together between covers and throw it at them.
SHERWOOD ANDERSON

On the whole, it is a flat time, and publishers have nothing to say to poets, regarding them as unprofitable people.
SIR HENRY TAYLOR (1800-1886)

The balance sheets of our great publishing houses would not be materially affected if they ceased from tomorrow the publication of poetry and literary criticism, and most publishers would rejoice to be relieved of the unprofitable burden or vain solicitations which such publication encourages.

HERBERT READ

The fact is that the intrinsic worth of the book, play or whatever the author is trying to sell is the least, last factor in the whole transaction. There is probably no other trade in which there is so little relationship between profits and actual value, or into which sheer chance so largely enters.

GEORGE BERNARD SHAW

I draw up my own agreements with Messrs. MacMillan, who also, as a matter of courtesy—and subject, of course, to a considerable use of the privilege—give me unlimited free copies. If any author is really worth publishing, he can get these terms from any decent publishing house.

H. G. WELLS

Until the manuscript is delivered, power is shared. When the manuscript enters the publishing process, power shifts to the publisher. It is the publisher who decides how the book is presented to the public.

TED SOLOTAROFF

Be persistent. Editors change; tastes change; editorial markets change. Too many beginning writers give up too easily.

JOHN JAKES

Publishers will tell you, with their tongue in their cheek, that every manuscript which reaches their office is faithfully read, but they are not to be believed. At least fifteen out of twenty manuscripts can be summarily rejected, usually with safety. There may be a masterpiece among them, but it is a thousand to one against.

MICHAEL JOSEPH

Another illusion, seldom entertained by competent authors, is that the publisher's readers and others are waiting to plagiarize their work. I think it may be said that the more worthless the manuscript, the greater the fear of plagiarism.

STANLEY UNWIN

The publisher is a middleman, he calls the tune to which the whole of the rest of the trade dances; and he does so because he pays the piper.

GEOFFREY FABER

It is a meretricious view that writers and editors are "creative" and that production and sales are 'servicing'. Creativity has to be at the heart of all publishing.

PETER MAYER

Publishing is a very mysterious business. It is hard to predict what kind of sale or reception a book will have, and advertising seems to do very little good.

THOMAS WOLFE, in a letter to his mother

A small press is an attitude, a kind of anti-commerciality. The dollars come second, the talent and the quality of the writing come first. If the presses wanted to make money, they'd be out there selling cookbooks.

BILL HENDERSON

To write books is easy, it requires only pen and ink and the ever-patient paper. To print books is a little more difficult, because genius so often rejoices in illegible handwriting. To read books is more difficult still, because of the tendency to go to sleep. But the most difficult task of all that a mortal man can embark on is to sell a book.

from a poem by FELIX DAHN, paraphrased by
Sir Stanley Unwin

Anyone can sell. The secret is to have 50,000 books in your basement.

MARY ELLEN PINKHAM

It is easy to become a publisher but difficult to remain one.

MICHAEL JOSEPH

I should be sorry to think it was the publishers themselves that got up this entire little flutter to enable them to unload a book that was taking too much room in their cellars, but you can never tell what a publisher will do. I have been one myself.

MARK TWAIN, when *Huckleberry Finn* was banned in Omaha.

They just wanted to sell books, that's all they wanted to do. It wasn't about anything, and I knew that—I figured they had to know that, they were in the business of it.

BOB DYLAN

You often get this awful feeling that they know your book is not going to sell and they begin to make you feel it; they take no trouble with it and you feel that if you put down Jesus Christ, somebody is going to say "who he" in brackets after it.

DANIEL HALPERN

My family used to tell everybody that the first word I said was 'book.' I tell everybody that my second word was 'terms.' And by the time I was three, I could spell "co-op advertising".

LEN RIGGIO, CEO of B. Dalton Booksellers

I object to publishers: the one service they have done me is to teach me to do without them. They combine commercial rascality with artistic touchiness and pettishness, without being either good business men or fine judges of literature. All that is necessary in the production of a book is an author and a bookseller, without the intermediate parasite.

GEORGE BERNARD SHAW

Publishers are demons, there's no doubt about it.

WILLIAM JAMES

And it does no harm to repeat, as often as you can, 'Without me the literary industry would not exist: the publishers, the agents, the sub-agents, the sub-sub-agents, the accountants, the libel lawyers, the departments of literature, the professors, the theses, the books of criticism, the reviewers, the book pages—all this vast and proliferating edifice is because of this small, patronized, put-down and underpaid person.'

DORIS LESSING

He wrote the books, then he died.

WILLIAM FAULKNER, on what a writer's obituary should read.

When I am dead,
I hope it may be said:
"His sins were scarlet, but his books were read."

HILAIRE BELLOC

I always wanted to write a book that ended with the
word "mayonnaise."

RICHARD BRAUTIGAN

When writers die they become books, which is, after
all, not too bad an incarnation.

JORGE LUIS BORGES

. . . of making many books there is no end.

ECCLESIASTES 12:12

INDEX

FOR THE BEST IN PAPERBACKS, LOOK FOR THE

In every corner of the world, on every subject under the sun, Penguin represents quality and variety—the very best in publishing today.

For complete information about books available from Penguin—including Pelicans, Puffins, Peregrines, and Penguin Classics—and how to order them, write to us at the appropriate address below. Please note that for copyright reasons the selection of books varies from country to country.

In the United Kingdom: For a complete list of books available from Penguin in the U.K., please write to *Dept E.P., Penguin Books Ltd, Harmondsworth, Middlesex, UB7 0DA.*

In the United States: For a complete list of books available from Penguin in the U.S., please write to *Dept BA, Penguin*, Box 120, Bergenfield, New Jersey 07621-0120.

In Canada: For a complete list of books available from Penguin in Canada, please write to *Penguin Books Canada Ltd, 10 Alcorn Avenue, Suite 300, Toronto, Ontario, Canada M4V 3B2.*

In Australia: For a complete list of books available from Penguin in Australia, please write to the *Marketing Department, Penguin Books Ltd, P.O. Box 257, Ringwood, Victoria 3134.*

In New Zealand: For a complete list of books available from Penguin in New Zealand, please write to the *Marketing Department, Penguin Books (NZ) Ltd, Private Bag, Takapuna, Auckland 9.*

In India: For a complete list of books available from Penguin, please write to *Penguin Overseas Ltd, 706 Eros Apartments, 56 Nehru Place, New Delhi, 110019.*

In Holland: For a complete list of books available from Penguin in Holland, please write to *Penguin Books Nederland B.V., Postbus 195, NL-1380AD Weesp, Netherlands.*

In Germany: For a complete list of books available from Penguin, please write to *Penguin Books Ltd, Friedrichstrasse 10-12, D-6000 Frankfurt Main I, Federal Republic of Germany.*

In Spain: For a complete list of books available from Penguin in Spain, please write to *Longman, Penguin España, Calle San Nicolas 15, E-28013 Madrid, Spain.*

In Japan: For a complete list of books available from Penguin in Japan, please write to *Longman Penguin Japan Co Ltd, Yamaguchi Building, 2-12-9 Kanda Jimbocho, Chiyoda-Ku, Tokyo 101, Japan.*

p. 39   adult = obsolete child

p. 44   lightning / lighting bug